frontispiece:
Matisse in his studio at the Regina,
Nice-Cimiez. Winter 1952-53.
Photo Hélène Adant, Paris.

THE LAST WORKS
OF HENRI MATISSE

Large Cut Gouaches

BY MONROE WHEELER.   THE MUSEUM OF MODERN ART, NEW YORK

IN COLLABORATION WITH THE ART INSTITUTE OF CHICAGO

AND THE SAN FRANCISCO MUSEUM OF ART

DISTRIBUTED BY D̶ ̶ ̶ ̶ ̶ ̶ID COMPANY, INC., GARDEN CITY, NEW YORK

Library of Congress Catalogue Card Number 61-18453

© The Museum of Modern Art, 1961. 11 West 53 St.,
N.Y. 19

Printed in the U.S.A. by the John B. Watkins Co.,
New York

Color plates printed in France by Mourlot Frères,
Paris

ACKNOWLEDGMENTS

On behalf of the Trustees of The Museum of Modern Art, The Art Institute of Chicago, and the San Francisco Museum of Art, I wish to express our particular gratitude to Madame Marguerite Duthuit-Matisse and Messrs. Jean and Pierre Matisse for their generous assistance without which an American showing of their father's last work would not have been possible. Our sincere thanks and appreciation are also extended to the following persons whose gracious advice and cooperation greatly facilitated our undertaking:

Mr. Henri Seyrig, Director of the Museums of France; Mr. Jean Cassou, Chief Curator of the Musée National d'Art Moderne, Paris, and its Curator, Mr. Bernard Dorival; Mr. Philippe Erlanger, Director of the Association Française d'Action Artistique; Mr. Edouard Morot-Sir, Cultural Counselor of the French Embassy; Mr. Jean Medecin, Deputy and Mayor of Nice; Mr. Jacques Thirion, Director of the Museums of the City of Nice; Mr. E. Tériade; Miss Lydia Delectorskaya; Mr. François Mathey, Curator of the Musée des Arts Décoratifs, Paris; Governor Nelson A. Rockefeller; Mr. E. Beyeler; Mr. Douglas MacAgy, Director of The Dallas Museum for Contemporary Arts; Madame Hélène Adant, who has provided all the photographs except those on pages 8, 14, 16, 43; Mr. Alfred H. Barr, Jr.; Mr. Peter Selz; Mr. William C. Seitz; Mr. William S. Lieberman; Mrs. Harry A. Woodruff; Miss Alicia Legg; Mr. Fernand Mourlot, and Mr. Maurice Lefebvre-Foinet.

Monroe Wheeler, *Director of the Exhibition*

EXHIBITION DATES:

The Museum of Modern Art, New York:
   Oct. 17—Dec. 3, 1961

The Art Institute of Chicago:
   Jan. 10—Feb. 13, 1962

San Francisco Museum of Art:
   March 12—April 22, 1962

Bedroom of Matisse, 1951. On wall: designs for chasubles for the Vence Chapel. Above the fireplace: Picasso's *Landscape, Vallauris,* 1950. Beside the fireplace: Matisse's last painting, *Woman in Yellow Blouse,* 1951. Photo Hélène Adant.

The exhibition which this book accompanies might be called a sequel to the large Matisse retrospective presented in 1951-1952,[1] when The Museum of Modern Art published not only a catalogue but Alfred H. Barr, Jr.'s monumental and definitive study, *Matisse: His Art and His Public*. Matisse had already produced a number of his important cut-and-pasted gouache compositions, which were exhibited at that time: *Beasts of the Sea, The Thousand and One Nights,* eight designs for stained-glass windows and a set of patterns for chasubles for the Chapel of the Rosary of the Dominican Nuns in Vence.[2] But Matisse went on with this medium until his death in 1954, varying and developing the technique on a larger and larger scale, imbuing it with a subtlety and depth of meaning which no one had foreseen when he began working in this way. Therefore it has seemed imperative to exhibit this last chapter of his lifework.

Over and above our desire to make known in this country every aspect of Matisse's work, these audacious final productions have a particular significance with reference to certain early achievements and to his art as a whole. He was an artist of the greatest resourcefulness in his several media, and he had always shown a particular interest in, and mastery of, two-dimensional representation: the use of flat or cursorily modeled color bounded by a dark peremptory line or by a blank space on the canvas or the page, not for decorative effect, but to give a magical illusion of entire and rounded form, in true perspective and in three dimensions.

A very impressive prefiguration of these cut gouache compositions appears in the *Interior with Eggplants* in the Grenoble museum, painted in Collioure in 1911. Executed in tempera, a medium which like gouache lends itself to effects of flatness, it portrays a room not only carpeted but bordered by large flowers, subdivided around an arabesque screen, with stylizations of a window and a mirror and a fireplace, and pictures within the picture; and in the center of all this, on a table with a leaf-patterned cloth, the vegetables which gave it its title. A Chinese proverb says that to dream of three eggplants

[1] Co-Sponsors: The Museum of Modern Art, New York; The Cleveland Museum of Art; The Art Institute of Chicago; San Francisco Museum of Art.

[2] In 1953 and in 1955 The Museum of Modern Art acquired by purchase and gift five of these silk vestments and a sixth unfinished one.

Interior with Eggplants. (1911). Tempera, 82¾ " x 96⅛ ". Musée de Peinture et de Sculpture, Grenoble.

is a sign of happiness. Matisse had not heard of this until 1952 when Jean Leymarie, the curator of the Grenoble museum, informed him of it.[3] Matisse expressed pleasure at having discovered, by chance or by instinct, this bit of ancient Chinese lore, and agreed that in concept and idiom the Grenoble picture was prophetic of the art of his old age.

Matisse's first known use of scissors was in 1931, at the age of sixty-two, when he undertook the important decorations for Dr. Albert C. Barnes's gallery in Merion, Pennsylvania. As a means of experimentation in the placement of forms and in linear and voluminous

[3]Jean Leymarie, "Les grandes gouaches découpées de Matisse à la Kunsthalle de Berne," *Quadrum VII,* Brussels, 1959.

relationships, he made and used movable paper cutouts. In subsequent years, in much the same way, he designed covers for the periodical, *Verve*, for catalogues of exhibitions of his work, for the dust-wrapper of Alfred Barr's volume, for posters, ballet sets and costumes, for tapestries, rugs and ceramics as well as the liturgical raiment and windows above mentioned, and for the picture book, *Jazz*, with a text in his own handwriting. To quote Mr. Barr, "Unlike the cubists who used scraps rescued from wastepaper baskets or the dadaists who cut up old mail-order catalogues, Matisse was not even satisfied with the best commercial colored papers: he had his own papers painted with gouaches of his own choosing and then proceeded with his scissors" (Bibl. 1). In the case of *Jazz*, as specified by Matisse in his text, "the images in vivid and violent tones have resulted from crystallizations of memories of the circus, popular tales or travel"; and the purpose of his writing was to clarify the reactions to these "chromatic and rhythmic improvisations." (Cat. No. 36)

Toward the end of his life, in ill health and unable to work at his easel, he made a virtue and a method of his infirmity; defiant of bodily weakness, he proceeded to extend this seemingly small-scale medium to monumental dimensions: *The Swimming Pool* is over fifty feet in length.

These final brilliantly painted and cutout gouaches epitomize Matisse's art in his most exuberant and felicitous vein. Early and late, he clearly stated his principles and objectives. First and foremost he believed in indefatigable preparation and experiment, not for virtuosity's sake, but to arrive at simplicity and forthrightness in the end. "The performance of the acrobat appears easy and relaxed," he said in an interview with Léon Degand, "but let us not lose sight of the long preliminary ordeal which enables him to give this effect. It is the same in painting. With hard work, the mastery of one's medium should pass from the conscious to the subconscious; only then can one successfully give an impression of spontaneity. . . . An artist is an explorer. He has to begin by self-discovery and by observation of his own procedure. After that he must not feel under any constraint. But, above all, he must never be too easily satisfied with what he has done." (Bibl. 5)

Whatever Matisse's subject matter, representational or symbolic, he aimed at the quintessential and the universal; he reminded us that the great differences of form in the foliage of a tree do not keep us from recognizing its common quality; that "no leaf of a fig tree is identical with any of its other leaves; each has a form of its own, but they all proclaim: Fig tree!". (Cat. No. 36)

When he came to the last cycle of his creative life, Matisse was aware of its being a culmination rather than a change. "There is no break between my painting and my cutouts. Only, with something more of the abstract and the absolute, I have arrived at a distillation of form. . . . Of this or that object which I used to present in all its complexity in space, I now keep only the sign which suffices, necessary for its existence in its own form, for the composition as I conceive it." (Bibl. 11)

In Matisse's view, art had but three aspects: color, not as a means of representation but for its own sake, to decorate and to express emotion; exact and unique draughtsmanship; and three-dimensional form inspired by sculpture. "The paintings of the impressionists, constructed with pure colors, proved to the next generation that these colors, while they might be descriptive of particular objects or phenomena of nature, have also the inherent power of affecting the feelings of those who look at them. . . . A blue, for instance, accompanied by the shimmer of its complementaries, acts upon the inner sensibility like the sudden stroke of a gong. The same with red and yellow; the artist must be able to strike them when he needs to." (Bibl. 14)

"Cutting colored papers permits me to draw in the color. For me it is a matter of simplification. Instead of establishing a contour, and then filling it with color—the one modifying the other—I draw directly in the color. . . . This guarantees a precise union of the two processess; they become one." (Bibl. 10)

In these last works, having been a colorist all his life, Matisse still pits one vivid color against another, with an unerring sense of beauty and youthful vigor. Having been a sculptor, he carves surface and space and attaches it with pins and paste. A draughtsman above all, he draws perhaps better than ever with the two matched blades of steel; biting the form as a wild beast might seize upon its prey; caressing the contour, though with hard metal, as gently as a lover's hand; urging it along to its culmination in a recognizable image.

The Creole Dancer (plate A) of June, 1950 seems to hark back to the fabrics and fashions of the twenties, with featherlike forms in green, blue and white on a patch-work background of darker and warmer colors. The famous standing figure of Zulma (page 14) in the Copenhagen museum, also early in the series, relates to Matisse's renderings of the female body in the forties, the body composed of a vertical strip of sunburned flesh on a monumental form of shadowy blue. That same year he undertook an immense and complex composition inspired by The Thousand and One Nights (pages 18-19). Scheherazade, the king's favorite who distracted him from putting her to death

10

by telling him stories night after night, "when she saw the first light of dawn, held her tongue discreetly." Matisse tells us this in cutout letters in the upper right-hand corner of the composition. It consists of five aligned rectangles, semi-abstract, surrounded by leaf forms, some like hands, some like hearts.

Another major composition, *Sorrows of the King* (plates F, G) two years later, derives from the literature of the Near East. At about the same time he had considered illustrating The Song of Songs, but apparently this king is David, the harpist, rather than his son, Solomon. The rhapsodical royal figure in three greens, a guitar-form of orange with white hands playing above it; on the right, a large archaic harp, black and white with golden strings; and in the nocturnal blue overhead, and in a bright space like a window on the right, miscellaneous small yellow shapes suggestive of the harp music.

In 1951, having terminated the Vence chapel, he produced two other stained-glass windows, for E. Tériade and for Time Inc., powerful compartmentalized designs: *Chinese Fish* (plate K) one white and one gold in green water, with an ambiance of tile-like patterns; and *Nuit de Noël* (plate J) with white stars, black stars, and one great yellow star.

The year 1952 was one of Matisse's most productive periods. He began with a great series of nudes, one evolving from the other as in musical counterpoint, with meaningful similarities, and magical changes. In one called *Venus* (plate L) the female figure, simplified to an extreme degree, is nothing but white paper between two large pieces of blue; the goddess half hidden in a night of lapis. Another standing figure (plate H) is in five parts: two upraised arms, the head and torso in one piece, and two long and strong legs joined with intervening white.

There is a homogeneous group of seated nudes (pages 22-23; plate M) with one knee up and one arm overhead, differentiated with a subtlety and virtuosity which astound us; the same pose lovingly and tirelessly observed on successive days or from hour to hour.

On one occasion he miscalculated the amount of blue paper he was going to need, and completed the legs with green paper, entitling it *Blue Nude with Green Stockings* (page 25). The upper body of another seated nude, on bright yellow, *The Frog* (plate E) consists of three almost identical circles enclosed in roughly shaped uplifted arms. There are also female acrobats, bent over backwards (page 28); amphora bearers (page 29; plate P); and a superb dancing or running figure, with streaming hair (plate I).

In due course, he incorporated these blue female figures in an important mural

11

12

Designs for Chasubles and Church Vestments
for the Vence Chapel. (c.1950).
Gouache on cut-and-pasted paper
(for execution in appliquéd cloth).
Musée Matisse, Nice-Cimiez, France.

13

Zulma. 1950. Gouache and crayon on cut-and-pasted paper, 7'9¾" x 52⅜". Statens Museum for Kunst, Copenhagen.

design, *Women and Monkeys* (pages 26-27) upon a strip of white with seven pome-granates, flanked by two sinuous anthropoids. Then the largest of all his designs, intended for a wall ceramic, *The Swimming Pool* (pages 32-33; plates B, C), also on a white strip, but mounted on a light brown expanse of raw canvas, with various forms leaping, diving or floating indolently on their backs, and sometimes, as Jacques Lassaigne has remarked (Bibl. 9), rising out of the white into the brown with the joyous vitality of dolphins springing from the waves.

In two compositions of 1953 Matisse came closer to outright abstraction than in any of his earlier work. *The Snail* (page 38) is an array of unequal rectangles, black, magenta, orange and yellow, turning on an axis of green against white. An important part of *Souvenir of Oceania* (plate D) is just draughtsmanship, black on white suggestive of nudities. There is also a hinted body, white bounded by blue, as in *Venus* above-mentioned, and a mysterious incomplete silhouette of yellow; and all this is assailed from above and from the right by vigorously descending rectangles.

By way of subject-matter he often contented himself with leaves or flowers, a heavily curving, severely pruned vine of blue with variegated foliage (page 42); a bed of ivy (page 35); wild poppies in the midst of fruit (pages 36-37). *Acanthuses* (page 39) has lances of green and yellow thrusting into the air over a bank of disparate, loosely spaced vegetation.

Throughout this last chapter of his life, as in all his previous work, Matisse delighted in the alternation between purely linear representation and the frankest pattern-making in juxtaposed, violent, almost savage color. One of the largest and most resplendent of the mural decorations epitomizes this dual interest; a polyptych eleven feet high and thirty-three feet wide, *Large Decoration with Masks* (pages 40-41; plates N, O); which is bounded at either side with uprights of blue, with a central section of huge blue flowers on white. The right and left areas are filled with a four-square pattern of many-hued flowers and fruit, in the midst of which hang, moon-like, two idealized faces in black and white.

The visual imagery of the windows and the chasubles of the Vence chapel is also mainly floral, vegetal and tropical—further variations on his long-chosen half-symbolic themes.

Matisse's last design, completed only a few days before his death on November 3, 1954, was for a rose window in the Union Church of Pocantico Hills, New York (page 43) in memory of Abby Aldrich Rockefeller, a founder of The Museum of Modern Art. Recalling the support given him in his early years by four members of the Stein family of San Francisco, it is gratifying that the final accomplishment of his prodigious career should have been commissioned by another American family whom he knew and admired.

At first, because of the size and innate fragility of all these works, it seemed impossible to exhibit them on this side of the Atlantic. But with the devoted and generous cooperation of the artist's daughter and sons, and of the Musée National d'Art Moderne in Paris and the museums of Nice, the difficulties were overcome.

During his lifetime, Matisse gave a number of his pictures to the city of Nice, and his wife, after his death, expressed a desire to have her own collection of her husband's works placed there in a museum. Their children having agreed to this, the municipality made available the principal floor of a chateau in the suburb of Cimiez, between the Roman arena and the famous grove of transplanted ancient olive trees, a few steps from Matisse's residence and from his tomb. There, in due course, the Matisse Museum will be opened to the public.

left: Study for the door of the Tabernacle of the *Chapelle du Rosaire des Dominicaines de Vence*, Alpes-Maritimes, France. (c. 1950).

opposite: *Beasts of the Sea.* 1950. Gouache on cut-and-pasted paper, 9'7" x 60¼". Private collection.

les bêtes de la mer...

H. matisse 50

17

The Thousand and One Nights. 1950.
Gouache on cut-and-pasted paper,
57″ x 12′6½″. Private collection.

19

Vegetables. 1952. Gouache
on cut-and-pasted paper,
69″ x 32¼″. Private collection.

Snow Flowers. 1951. Gouache
on cut-and-pasted paper,
68″ x 32″. Private collection.

21

22

H MATISSE 52

from left to right:

Seated Blue Nude, No. 2. 1952.
Gouache on cut-and-pasted paper,
45¾" x 35". Private collection.

Seated Blue Nude, No. 3. 1952.
Gouache on cut-and-pasted paper,
45¾" x 32". Private collection.

Seated Blue Nude, No. 4. 1952.
Gouache on cut-and-pasted paper,
40½" x 30¼". Private collection.

Blue Nude Skipping Rope. (1952).
Gouache on cut-and-pasted paper,
57″ x 38½″. Private collection.

24

Blue Nude with Green Stockings. (1952).
Gouache on cut-and-pasted paper,
8'6¼" x 66". Private collection.

25

26

Women and Monkeys. (1952).
Gouache on cut-and-pasted paper,
28″ x 9′4¼″. Private collection.

28

Woman with Amphora and Pomegranates. (1952).
Gouache on cut-and-pasted
paper, 7′11¼″ x 37¾″.
Private collection.

opposite: *Acrobats.*
(1952). Gouache and
crayon on cut-and-pasted
paper, 7′ x 6′9½″.
Private collection.

29

Bather in the Reeds. (1952). Gouache on cut-and-pasted paper, 46½ " x 67¼ ". Private collection.

opposite: *Sailboat.* (1952) Gouache on cut-and-pasted paper, 56¼ " x 44". Private collection.

31

The Swimming Pool. Design
for wall ceramic. (1952).
Gouache on cut-and-pasted
paper, 7'6½" x 53'11¾".
Private collection.

34

Ivy in Flower. Design for a stained glass window. 1953. Gouache on cut-and-pasted paper, 9'4" x 9'4". The Dallas Museum for Contemporary Arts. Gift of the Albert and Mary Lasker Foundation.

opposite: *Nude with Oranges.* (1953). Gouache on cut-and-pasted paper, 60" x 42". Private collection.

36

Wild Poppies. Design for a stained glass window.
(1953). Gouache and crayon on cut-and-pasted paper,
31½″ x 11'2½″. Private collection.

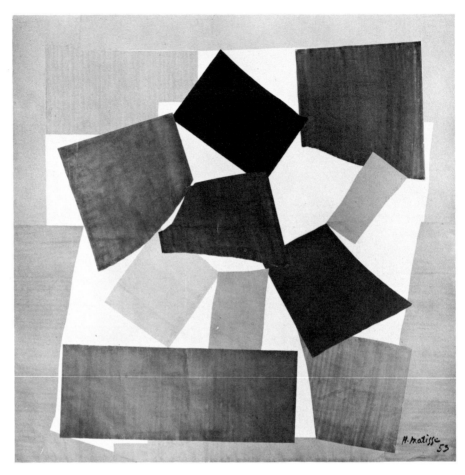

The Snail. 1953. Gouache on cut-and-pasted paper, 9'4¾" x 9'5". Private collection.

opposite: *The Acanthuses.* Design for wall ceramic. (1953). Gouache on cut-and-pasted paper. 10'2½" x 11'6¼". Galerie E. Beyeler, Basel.

39

40

Large Decoration with Masks.
Design for wall ceramic. 1953.
Gouache on cut-and-pasted paper,
11'7¾" x 32'10¾". Private collection.

The Vine. Design for a stained glass window. (1953). Gouache on cut-and-pasted paper, 8'8¼" x 37". Private collection.

opposite: *Design for Rose Window, Union Church of Pocantico Hills, New York in Memory of Abby Aldrich Rockefeller.* (1954). Gouache on cut-and-pasted paper, 6'4⅜" in diameter. Collection Governor Nelson A. Rockefeller, New York.

43

SELECTED BIBLIOGRAPHY

1 BARR, ALFRED H., Jr. Matisse: His Art and His Public, New York, Museum of Modern Art, 1951. *Bibliography.*

2 BERNE. KUNSTHALLE. Henri Matisse, 1950-1954: Les Grandes Gouaches Découpées. 1959. *Preface by Franz Meyer. Catalogue of exhibit also shown at the Stedelijk Museum, Amsterdam, 1960.*

3 COURTHION, PIERRE. Papiers découpées d'Henri Matisse. *XXᵉ Siècle* no. 6, 1956.

4 COUTURIER, MARIE ALAIN. Ronchamp-Vence. Paris, Editions du Cerf, 1955. *Texts also by L. B. Rayssiguier, A.-M. Cocagnac.*

5 DEGAND, LEON. Matisse à. Paris. *Les Lettres Françaises* Oct. 6, 1945.

6 DIEHL, GASTON. Henri Matisse. New York, Universe Books, 1958. *Translation of the Tisné edition (Paris, 1954). Bibliography.*

7 DUTHUIT, GEORGES & REVERDY, PIERRE. The Last Works of Henri Matisse, 1950-1954. New York, Harcourt, Brace, 1958. *American edition of Verve nos. 35-36 (Paris, 1958).*

8 ESCHOLIER, RAYMOND, Matisse from the Life. London, Faber & Faber, 1960. *Translation of Matisse, ce Vivant (Paris, Fayard, 1956).*

9 LASSAIGNE, JACQUES. Matisse. Geneva, Skira, 1959. *Translated from the French. Bibliography.*

10 LEJARD, ANDRE. [Matisse]. *Amis de l'Art* Oct. 1951.

11 LUZ, MARIA. Témoinages: Henri Matisse. *XXᵉ Siècle* no. 2, 1952.

12 PARIS, MUSEE DES ARTS DECORATIFS. Henri Matisse. Les Grandes Gouaches Decoupées. 1961. *Exhibition catalogue with preface by Jacques Lassaigne. Bibliography.*

13 POCANTICO HILLS. UNION CHURCH. The Abby Aldrich Rockefeller Memorial Window. [1956]

14 VENCE. CHAPELLE DU ROSAIRE DES DOMINICAINES. Chapelle du Rosaire des Dominicaines de Vence par Henri Matisse. 1951.

15 VERDET, ANDRE. Prestiges de Matisse. Paris, Emile-Paul, 1952.

Works marked with an asterisk are illustrated. Dates enclosed in parentheses do not appear on the works of art. All works are in gouache on cut-and-pasted paper unless otherwise noted. In dimensions, height precedes width.

1 *The Dancer*. (1938) 30 x 24″. Private collection.

* 2 *Creole Dancer*. June 1950. Gouache and crayon on cut-and-pasted paper, 6′8¾″ x 47¼″. Museums of the City of Nice, France. Ill. pl. A of color section.

* 3 *The Thousand and One Nights*. 1950. 57″ x 12′6½″. Private collection. Ill. pp. 18-19.

* 4 *Beasts of the Sea*. 1950. 9′7″ x 60¼″. Private collection. Ill. p. 17.

* 5 *Snow Flowers*. 1951. 68 x 32″. Private collection. Ill. p. 21.

* 6 *Chinese Fish*. Design for a stained glass window. 1951. Gouache and crayon on cut-and-pasted paper, 6′3¼″ x 35¾″. Private collection. Ill. pl. K of color section.

* 7 *Vegetables*. 1952. 69 x 32¼″. Private collection. Ill. p. 20.

* 8 *Nuit de Noël*. Design for a stained glass window. 1952. 10′7″ x 53½″. The Museum of Modern Art, New York. Gift of Time Inc. Ill. pl. J of color section.

* 9 *Sorrows of the King*. 1952. 9′7¼″ x 12′8″. Musée National d'Art Moderne, Paris. Ill. pls. F–G of color section.

*10 *Standing Blue Nude*. (1952). 44½ x 29″. Private collection. Ill. pl. H of color section.

*11 *Blue Nude Skipping Rope*. (1952). 57 x 38½″. Private collection. Ill. p. 24.

*12 *Blue Nude with Green Stockings*. (1952). 8′6¼″ x 66″. Private collection. Ill. p. 25.

*13 *Blue Nude, The Frog*. (1952). 55½ x 52¾″. Private collection. Ill. pl. E of color section.

*14 *Venus*. (1952). 39¾ x 30¼″. Private collection. Ill. pl. L of color section.

*15 *Blue Nude with Flowing Hair*. 1952. 42½ x 31½″. Private collection. Ill. pl. I of color section.

*16 *Seated Blue Nude, No. 1*. 1952. 41¾ x 30¾″. Private collection. Ill. pl. M of color section.

*17 *Seated Blue Nude, No. 2*. 1952. 45¾ x 35″. Private collection. Ill. p. 22.

*18 *Seated Blue Nude, No. 3*. 1952. 45¾ x 32″. Private collection. Ill. p. 22.

*19 *Seated Blue Nude, No. 4*, 1952. 40½ x 30¼″. Private collection. Ill. p. 23.

*20 *Acrobats*. (1952). Gouache and crayon on cut-and-pasted paper, 7′ x 6′9½″. Private collection. Ill. p. 28.

*21 *Bather in the Reeds*. (1952). 46½ x 67¼″. Private collection. Ill. p. 30.

*22 *Sailboat*. (1952). 56¼ x 44″. Private collection. Ill. p. 31.

*23 *Woman with Amphora and Pomegranates*. (1952). 7′11¼″ x 37¾″. Private collection. Ill. p. 29.

*24 *Woman with Amphora*. (1952). 64½ x 19″. Private collection. Ill. pl. P of color section.

*25 *The Swimming Pool.* Design for wall ceramic. (1952). 7'6½" x 53'11¾". Private collection. Ill. pls. B—C of color section (detail); pp. 32-33.

*26 *Women and Monkeys.* (1952). 28"x9'4¼". Private collection. Ill. pp. 26-27.

*27 *Nude with Oranges.* (1953). 60 x 42". Private collection. Ill. p. 34.

*28 *Large Decoration with Masks.* Design for wall ceramic. 1953. 11'7¾" x 32'10¾". Private collection. Ill. pls. N—O of color section (detail); pp. 40-41.

*29 *The Snail.* 1953. 9'4¾" x 9'5". Private collection. Ill. p. 38.

*30 *Souvenir of Oceania.* 1953. Gouache and crayon on cut-and-pasted paper, 9'4¾" x 9'4¾". Private collection. Ill. pl. D of color section.

*31 *Ivy in Flower.* Design for a stained glass window. 1953. 9'4" x 9'4". The Dallas Museum for Contemporary Arts. Gift of the Albert and Mary Lasker Foundation. Ill. p. 35.

*32 *The Acanthuses.* Design for wall ceramic. (1953). 10'2½" x 11'6¼". Galerie E. Beyeler, Basel, Ill. p. 39.

*33 *The Vine.* Design for a stained glass window. (1953). 8'8¼" x 37". Private collection. Ill. p. 42.

*34 *Wild Poppies.* Design for a stained glass window. (1953). Gouache and crayon on cut-and-pasted paper, 31½" x 11'2½". Private collection. Ill. pp. 36-37.

*35 *Design for Rose Window, Union Church of Pocantico Hills, New York, in Memory of Abby Aldrich Rockefeller.* (1954). 6'4⅜" in diameter. Collection Governor Nelson A. Rockefeller, New York. Ill. p. 43.

36 *Jazz.* (1947). Album of 20 pochoir plates in color (stencils), 16⅝ x 25⅝", with slight variations (sheet size). The Museum of Modern Art, New York. Gift of the artist.

*37-39 Three designs for Church Vestments for the *Chapelle du Rosaire des Dominicaines de Vence,* Alpes-Maritimes, France. For execution in appliquéd cloth. (c. 1950). Musée Matisse, Nice-Cimiez, France. Ill. pp. 12, 13.

40 Design for The Museum of Modern Art, New York Exhibition Catalogue. (1951). 10⅝ x 15¾". The Museum of Modern Art, New York.

41 Design for Jacket of *Matisse: His Art and His Public.* (1951). 10⅝ x 16⅞". The Museum of Modern Art, New York.

INDEX OF COLOR PLATES

The color reproductions in this volume were made by Fernand Mourlot in Paris. As in those made during the artist's lifetime, the brush strokes visible in the gouache paint of the originals have been omitted, Matisse having conceived the designs in pure flat hues. Dates enclosed in parentheses do not appear on the works of art. All works are in gouache on cut-and-pasted paper unless otherwise noted. In dimensions, height precedes width. M. W.

47

B-C

D

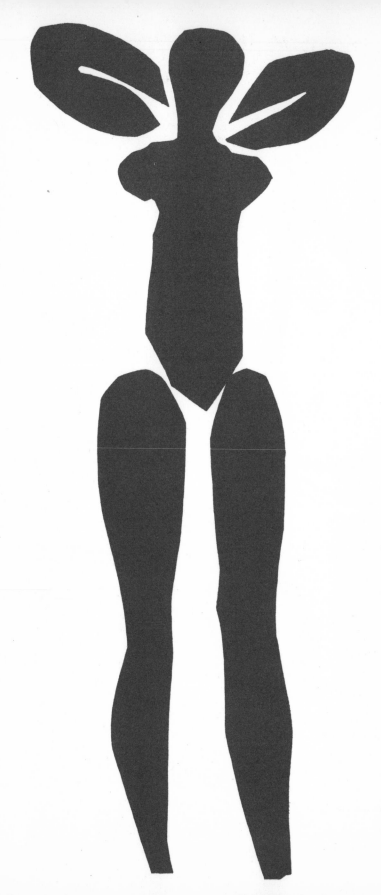

H

H.MATISSE 52

J

H. MATISSE 51

L

P